SAP SCM Interview Questions, Answers, and Explanations: SAP SCM Certification Review

SAPCOOKBOOK.COM

Please visit our website at www.sapcookbook.com

ISBN 1-933804-08-4

TABLE OF CONTENTS

SAP SCM Interview Questions, Answers, and Explanations: SAP SCM Certification Review

SAPCOOKBOOK

Equity Press

☞ Question 1

Question 1: APO DP planning book upload type

I have to upload data in the DP planning book from a legacy system. The different options available regarding the update type from this field are as follows:

OW1 - Overwrite Completely, First Period distribution
OW2 - Overwrite Completely, Consistent distribution
PW1 - First: Overwrite partially Period Distribution
PW2 - Overwrite partially: Consistent Distribution
DL1 - Delta Update: First Period Distribution
DL2 - Delta Update: Consistent Distribution

My question is where can I find the PUPDATE field in APO to specify the nature of update type for the DP planning book?

✍ Answer

You can do the following for update purposes:

1. Change this template: /SAPAPO/TS_PSTRU_SAMPLE_MD_GEN in order to load with zeros.

2. Use the flag [X] Ignore zero values.

3. Update the values in table: RSSGTPCLA.

☞ QUESTION 2

NEGATIVE VALUES REQUIRED FOR FORECASTING

I am using APO to forecast negative values, but I don't see any option in my forecast profiles to allow for negative values. There also seems to be a system setting that automatically changes negative values to zero, which leads me to believe that I can turn it off as well. How do I enable my forecast profiles to allow negative value settings?

✍ ANSWER

If you are working with APO 4.0, you can produce negative values in forecasting MLR. Working with logarithms is reasonable as well. That is, if you mean non-negatives with time series.

☞ QUESTION 3

Creating a new key figure for a planning book

I started adding a new key figure in the planning book in DP by using BW admin (rsa1) but it doesn't show in the interactive demand planning book. How do I create or add a new key figure in a planning book in DP?

I did try to go in /sapapo/msdp_admin and select my planning area to add new key figures in there but the system said that there are some active versions and that I can only go in display mode. How can I go in change mode?

✍ ANSWER

If you intend to do some calculations and do not intend to save that data after exiting the planning book, you can use auxiliary Key figures. Also, keep in mind that you can only change inactive planning areas.

This being said, BEFORE you begin, please ensure that you have a backup of your live cache and info cube information required to rebuild the planning area when you have finished.

You will then have to delete the time series objects against the planning area (right click on the planning area and select delete), this will delete ALL values in the planning area hence the backup that is required.

Once this has been done the symbol next to the planning

area should change from a green circle to a red square, you should now be able to make your changes.

When you have completed the changes you will have the pleasant task of uploading your data again.

I suggest that you try this several times in your DEV environment before being sure of moving onto QA and PRD.

☞ Question 4

Characteristic drilldown

In the data view of the planning book, we have a number of key figures. When I drill down by product, I get the first key figure and the product drilldown. From there, the next key figure appears and the list goes on.

I would like to swap the drilldown between the characteristics and the drilldown.

Is there a way to change the format so that I can drilldown by the product and show all key figures for each product instead?

✍ Answer

Take the following steps to reformat according to your specifications:

1. First, set up the macro to do this. In the macro use statement DRILL_DOWN and specify the level (Product). When you run the macro it will show you the options.

2. You will need to have your header row displayed, and a header button created (i.e. for your product). Also make sure to have selected more than one product from the drop-down (or details) menu. This is required before it will allow pivot sorting.

3. Lastly, right-click in the top left hand corner of the dataview and select Pivot Sorting. From here, you can proceed to reformat.

☞ Question 5

Choosing day in period for lc order in the DP to SNP order

We have a monthly bucket in DP and SNP. When forecast is transferred from DP to SNP, it is created as one live cache order on the first day of the period covering the month. Is there a way to change the transfer so that the forecast order is on the 3rd or 4th day of the period?

For Example:

>DP 01/2006 forecast 100;
>Transfer to SNP;
>Forecast order created for 01/01/2006;

Instead, we would like it to be created for 01/04/2006.

✍ Answer

You can do two things to make the changes. First option is to check the forecast horizon field in the SNP2 tab of the product master. The second option is, if you are using CTM and have one forecast a month, change the CTM time stream to weekly and aggregate the forecast to this period via the aggregation tab in CTM. From there, choose the CTM global configuration setting to middle of the period. CTM will then treat the forecast at the beginning of the month (FI period actually) as if it was on the Wednesday of the first week of the month, instead of Monday.

☞ Question 6

SCEM Triggers

What transaction is used to change the configuration of event handlers? How do I set the triggers of the event handlers to be inactive?

✍ Answer

Go to SPRO> Integration with other mySAP.com Components > Event Management Interface > Define Application interface> Define SAP EM interface functions. From there, you can set the triggers of the event handler.

☞ Question 7

Change Planned orders to Production orders

I was trying to convert planned orders created in APO to production orders in R/3. I have placed the transfer indicator in the orders and when I execute the transaction for transfer it says transfer has taken place but I still cannot find the orders in R/3. How do I effect the change?

✍ Answer

If you have the Im in place, proceed to check the r3 inbound and outbound queues for any blocks.

The R3 conversion to process orders would have caused a change in the order number so you can't find the same order number in R3.

☞ Question 8

Data load errors

I am getting the following errors in the data loads In APO Quality system during monitoring checks: This is a quality client copied system from the
APO production system.

1. There is no PSA for info source LISVCIT and source system AP900.

2. System error occurred (rfc call).

3. Activation of data records is terminated.

How do I fix these errors?

✍ Answer

First, check that the info package is not loading directly to the cube. Make sure that it is loading to PSA first before going to the cube.

With errors 2 and 3, there seems to be a problem with whichever system is calling your client, and you should talk to your basis team to rectify rfc errors.

☞ Question 9

Using Custom KF in Transfer Profiles in DP

We are using the Custom Key Figure in DP and I am using the same custom characteristic figure in the transfer profile for the transfer of forecast from APO to R/3. It is not getting transferred nor does it throw any error log, and the other settings are fine (Publication types etc). What I would like to know is if it is possible to use the Custom KF in the transfer profile? Or should we use 9AMATNR only for the transfer of forecast requirements?

✍ Answer

You can use the custom characteristics to replace product (9AMATNR) and location (9ALOCNO) in APO. However, you have to define those characteristics when you build the MPOS.

You can do this in the screen of Configuring POS using EXTRA-->Assign Prod/LOC.

This should solve your release problem.

☞ Question 10

Storage bucket profile

We are required to carry out storage bucket profile maintenance in Production system as the horizon of storage bucket profile is getting expired (data backup from planning area has already been taken into cubes). Can I transport it to production by defining a new storage bucket profile into the development system? Or do I have to define it in the Production system directly? If I can transport the storage bucket profile, what is the Tcode for that?

✍ Answer

You can use the standard transport connection for DP and SNP using the transaction /SAPAPO/TSOBJ. You will also have to transport the planning area from dev to Prod plus all the relevant details like POS, Storage buckets, and planning buckets. Planning books will also get transported if you do not remove them manually from the request.

From hereon, it's your call to transport these things or just change the storage buckets directly in production.

☞ Question 11

Sales History for DP

We are trying to remove the duplicate storage of sales history data in two places and the consequent system overheads of loads and other similar items. Is it always necessary to load sales history into APO or can it be stored in the central BW (non-APO) and referenced via a remote cube in APO?

✍ Answer

This should be possible using BAPI " PlanningBookAPS" and using the methods " GetDetail" and "ChangeKeyfigureValue".

Similarly, this procedure also works for uploading data from excel to live cache without using info cube.

☞ Question 12

Inputting a Macro Note

How can I enter or attach a note to a macro in APO 4.1 Macro Workbench or MacroBuilder?

✍ Answer

Note can be maintained by clicking Macro workbench -> Planning Book.

When you click this, window is split in two and you get all the macros available.

From here right click the macro, you will get the option to add a note to macro.

Then, choose the change mode of the planning book>Right Click on any value in the planning table>choose 'display notes'. From there, you will see the notes and be able to give your own notes too.

☞ Question 13

Tracking of ALERTS

We have a requirement to see and keep track which Alerts User was worked on.

For Example: we have 19 alerts and want to see on which alerts (the number of alerts) the user worked on and how many more remaining alerts he/she needs to conclude the work.

How do I track, monitor and identify these alerts?

✍ Answer

The alerts have status which tells you whether they have been processed or not. If you look at the alert monitor screen you will find that there is a prompt whether to accept the alerts or undo it. Therefore, your option is on 'alert' monitor screen. Meanwhile, 'alert' status is stored in a structure. You can easily do a little research and put these all together to fulfill your requirement.

☞ Question 14

Parameter conversion error

How can I resolve the parameter conversion error when running alerts?

✍ Answer

You can run a consistency check on the alert and then re-activate it.

☞ Question 15

Past Due Demands (Backorders) and APO Optimizer

We just started testing APO Optimizer v4.1 and have the following issue:

'THE OPTIMIZER IS IGNORING PAST DUE DEMANDS'

EXAMPLE: We have a Sales Order with due dates in the past. This shows up in the INITIAL column of the planning table (transaction SNP94). When we run the optimizer, it ignores these Sales Orders (and any other past due demands). This action results in Supply Shortages throughout the entire planning horizon.

Heuristics does consider past due demands. Unfortunately, it does not meet our needs for developing a constrained supply plan.

How can we fix this problem so that the APO optimizer will reflect Past Due Demands (Backorders)?

✍ Answer

There are some settings in the optimizer profile that are used when building the model to send to the optimizer. If the demands are not met when sending the optimizer model, a value needs to be passed so that the system can recognize that it is possible to build a pegging link, which can then be analyzed and incorporate a 'waiting' program for possible backorder delays.

☞ Question 16

SNP

If not using DP and PPDS, how does SNP Work? I understand that Demand Plan has to be fed to SNP in order for SNP to do short to mid term planning. I also assume that PPMs came thru PPDS and if not using PPDS, we can use PPMs as APO Master data. If my knowledge of R/3 is accurate, then I further assume that we can transfer the demand plan from R/3 to APO and then execute SNP. However, I am not sure if these assumptions are accurate. Am I on the right track? If not, can I have some inputs so I may adjust accordingly?

✍ Answer

These are some facts about SNP:

1. SNP has CTM, where you could actually use PP/DS PPMs.

2. For Heuristics you'd need SNP PPMs only if you have in-house production.

3. You can plan for Demand (as you said can be transferred from R/3) as well as sales orders, depending on the above 2 scenarios.

☞ Question 17

APO SNP

My CTM run produces no result. I have created PPMs and assigned them to a model.

I am using standard planning book 9ASNP94. I am able to see my resources having capacity of 8 hours a day and also initial demand with stock on hand for my products.

I didn't make many changes to the CTM engine (all I mentioned is VERSION) and selected all master data. The log does not show any errors.

What could be the problem?

✍ Answer

Check your master data selection. Incorrect master data selection reflects no errors in Evaluation and yet does not produce any planning results either.

☞ QUESTION 18

PPDS quantity alerts

I found the results of the PPDS quantity alerts to be difficult to interpret in a real time business situation. Is there a way for these alerts for receipts and requirements to be programmed so as to reflect actual shortage and surplus in terms of percentages?

✍ ANSWER

The PPDS alerts are based on the pegging situation of the requirements and receipts. You can change the pegging windows and the alert windows mode on the demand tab/ pegging sub tab. This will change the results significantly. In general, set a broad range on the pegging limits that lets the receipts peg to the requirements. Afterwards, set the alert limits to see if things are late or early. This should take care of your concern.

☞ QUESTION 19

How to CIF the PPM without operations

We have setup a subcontracting flow. However, I need to plan it in APO. I need to start from a DP forecast, in PPDS to create a subcontracted PR (I have the subcontracted info record in APO) I need a PPM with the BOM. But, I can't CIF the BOM (ProdVersion) since it doesn't contain an operation. Must a PPM always contain an operation? I don't need that operation in APO, for the simple reason that there are no activities (except for the handling), and the service cost is in the info record. I would like to know what the best way is to go about it.

Should I create a dummy WorkCenter, and some dummy activity, just for the sake of being able to CIF the PPM?

✍ ANSWER

Proceed to create a dummy, infinite resource and a master recipe with 1 phase with a fast duration e.g. 1,000/hr.

As the PPM is used for the BOM explosion, the details of the task list are irrelevant.

☞ Question 20

Complex Setup time calculation

We are trying to figure out how to handle a complex calculation of setup times. We are working in a metal mill industry and setup times depend on dimensions. This means that setup is a very big factor for increasing width, but zero for decreasing width. As far as I know it is not possible to model something like that using setup groups and setup keys because this could lead to an infinite number of combinations. If you also consider thickness or other characteristics like color and even process characteristics like temperature, then the whole thing gets too complicated to handle via setup keys. How can I find a simpler method to approach this and fulfill the requirement of setting up a program that will automatically set up complex time calculations?

✍ Answer

You might be interested in some SCM 5.0 developments where the system can generate its own composite matrices based on matrices that you enter for swaps between individual characteristic evaluations. I mean characteristic evaluations, not setup groups. In this development, you can maintain a setup matrix for setup swaps between thickness characteristics, and another for length.

The system can then generate a composite matrix that will have many more entries (but it saves you from doing it), and it's possible to specify that the composite swap should either be the max, sum or badi dependent value with regard to the individuals.

The system also generates its own 'setup group' which it applies to the order that can then be used to build the swap time for the order in planning.

There are some restrictions, and you'll need to contact SAP to get some consulting if you are interested in taking it further.

☞ Question 21

No Entry FOR bw_user in the table RSADMIN

I am maintaining a source system in the Administration workbench of the APO by the Menu Supply chain planning-Demand Planning-Basic setting-Administrator workbench. Once I create source system type Sap-r/3 Manual creation selection and selected the R/3 Destination and logical system name from the Popup menu, the system indicates 'No entry for BW_USER in the table RSADMIN is available'.

When I check for details, the following information is given:

'No entry for BW_USER in table RSADMIN available;
Message no. RSAR 059
Diagnosis: Missing entry in table RSADMIN
System Response: Process for creating a source system terminated.'

I then went to the table RSADMIN. It is having entry for BW_USER as

'Object BW_USER' and further indicated: 'Value ALLREMOTE'

When I need to maintain another entry in this table, I plan to load the data from Sap/r3 Info structure to APO Info cube. For this I am going to do the following setting:

Procedure: In Customizing> maintain Proposal for Users in the Source System:

BW Customizing Implementation Guide -> Business Information Warehouse ->

Connections to Other Systems -> Connection between SAP Systems and BW ->

Maintain Proposal for Users in the Source System (ALE Communication).

I am concerned though that I might encounter the same response from the system. How do I resolve this issue?

✍ ANSWER

Check for the following:

1. Verify if you have the BW_USER set up both for the R/3 system and the APO system. They need to have the same password set for both systems.

2. Double check if you do not have BWREMOTE user. If you don't have it, go create a remote user (in IMG) and that will fix the problem.

☞ Question 22

Location transfer via CIF

We have a new plant and we are trying to CIF to APO at CFM2 system. It is showing the error 'Location does not exist for external location number EF00, type 1001, BSG'. How do we correct this error?

✍ Answer

First thing to do is to make sure you assigned the correct logical system (R/3) to a business system group. Secondly, check the Planning version attached to the plant. It should reflect '000'.

☞ Question 23

Proportional Factor

I need to set the proportion factor between a pack size (level higher) and product for the entire forecasting period.

Example: Under pack size PK1 give 100% for product A for months 1, 2 and 3 and 100 % for product B for the remaining months. This will help me so that after every monthly forecasting run, the plan numbers are disaggregated to the correct product (i.e. the active one for that month).

I can make the changes directly to the proportional factor key figure to achieve the above result but the problem is that every month, the proportional factors will be regenerated (i.e. new sales month included) and because of this, the percentage settings will be lost.

Can anyone suggest a clean approach to handle this problem? I need for the end user to maintain this and not the IT maintenance team. If I need to use macros, can you please give details on how it should work (i.e. the logic)?

✍ Answer

There are two possible ways to approach this:

1. Create a new key figure that will hold proportional factors and make your changes in it. Then copy that to the proportional factors row using a copy macro. Every time you regenerate your prop factors, remember to run a background job that will rewrite the proportional factor based on the new prop factors row. Don't keep your

original prop factors row open to editing. Keeping the new proportional factors open to edit must be enough.

2. Another solution is to use a new Key Figure. Store values that you do not want APODPDANT to overwrite in this KF and allow manual editing for this. Then overwrite this MANUAL KF with APODPDANT with a mass job or interactive fashion. Write batch planning books with minimal rows and macros for the mass job.

☞ Question 24

Using fact sheet from one product to determine sales of another product

The sale of some of our products is based on the sale of another product. For example: a sale of product A will lead to 2 sales of product B. So we should not have to forecast product B since it will be derived from product A.

How do I factor this in APO DP so that forecasting should be automatic for product B?

✍ Answer

Check the DP BOMS. It might present some possible solutions.

☞ QUESTION 25

Global view of Demand

We have created demand planning areas for different regions in Europe, Americas, and Asia.

If I want to have a Global view of my demand, what do I need to do?

Is there a similar concept to a BW multicube available in APO, kind of a "Multi Planning Area" or something?

✍ ANSWER

You should only create one planning area for different regions. But since you have already created a Multiplan, copy the data from one planning area to another to be able to show them together in data views. Or extract to BW in different info cubes and create a multi cube on top.

☞ QUESTION 26

Deleting product master from APO

How can I mass permanent delete product master (not just set the deletion flag) from APO? I have tried to use BDC and done /sapapo/mat1> Mark for deletion but the result comes out to set the deletion flag as supposed to permanent delete when you do it manually. Is there another way to do it?

✍ ANSWER

After setting the deletion flag just use the report to delete product master.

Try this menu path:

Master Data > Product Master > “Delete Products” off the Extras tab within the Product Master.

☞ QUESTION 27

Product Interchange

We have activated product interchangeability function. We want to have a range of substitution (one to many or vice versa). For example: A -> B, C ->B with different validity from date. Currently, system is not permitted when we create substitution C->B. It states: 'Error occurred: Interchangeability not continuous'.
What does this mean?

✍ ANSWER

The problem might have occurred because the assumptions are not supported. PP/DS only supports linear super session chains. In a linear super session chain, each product in the super session chain can have only one predecessor and one successor. The products in a super session chain are therefore linked by 1:1 relationships. Super session chains in which a product has several successor products (1:N), or several products have one successor product (N:1) are not permitted.

☞ Question 28

Creating PPMs in APO

I am trying to create PPMs in APO but then I am not able to understand as to how to satisfy this requirement. Is there a way to create PPMs manually in APO without getting anything transferred from R/3?

✍ Answer

If you have the products and the resources created in APO then you can create a plan (PPM).

First, you need to create the master data product and location manually. Then you can be able to create PPM manually, or get the master data CIF ed. One prerequisite of the PPM is having the master data.

☞ Question 29

No AUTOLOG File

We have installed SCM 4.1 on windows 64 bits (live cache 7.5).

I noted that there is no AUTOLOG file on operating system.

I have defined AUTOLOG Medium and it is in status AUTOLOG ON, but there is no file on operating system.

DEVLog is 2GB and LOG_SEGMENT_SIZE is 85333.

I think there is not a lot of activity on this system (it is not yet in production life).

But why there is no file on operating system?
Must I reduce LOG_SEGMENT_SIZE?
What problem could it generate?

I do a DATA backup one time by day and LOG backup 3 times by day.

I think when I do a LOG backup (and stop AUTOLOG before and restart it after), the log is empty? (And data are put in DATA?)

So may be it is normal there is no file in AUTOLOG.

Is it a problem for a restoration of warm backup?

✍ ANSWER

You will only get a log when the LOG is filled or if you force it to write it on logs. To force a log switch:

DBMCLI -d LCA -u control, control -uUTL -c autolog_off
DBMCLI -d LCA -u control, control -uUTL -c autolog_on

Or:

Create a media:
dbmcli -u control,control medium_put LOGS X:\LOGS FILE LOG 0 8 YES

Start backup on disk:
DBMCLI -d LCA -u control, control -uUTL -c autolog_off
DBMCLI -d LCA -u control, control -uUTL -c backup_start LOGS
DBMCLI -d LCA -u control, control -uUTL -c autolog_on

☞ Question 30

Forecasting profile

We are now in the process of testing various history data models to see what forecast APO will give us. So far we were not impressed with the auto models. Most of the time, they are just giving us constant models. Meanwhile, the history data clearly shows a trend and/or seasonality.

How we can make the forecast more accurate and reflective of relevant trends to enable the auto models to show it?

✍ Answer

Forecast models in APO are just the Statistical tools to help you arrive at forecast. So try playing with the forecast parameters for better accuracy

In case of Auto Model 2, try the following:

- Use an appropriate forecast horizon (> 2 years) if you are having a 1 year seasonal cycle;
- Clean the data to get rid of the known values of overselling or underselling (Promotions/Stock outs);
- Use APO outlier correction and sigma value of 1.25;

In case if you are not satisfied with the APO forecast values you can also use some external forecast models and bring the data back to APO using the User exits.

☞ Question 31

Selection ID in macro

I am in need of a selection ID in macro to send the information or save the information in a z table. The objective for this is to essentially monitor which selection ids are being used and by whom, in the interactive planning. How do I fetch a selection ID in macro?

✍ Answer

The solution is simple enough. Use table /SAPAPO/TS_SELKO.

☞ QUESTION 32

Live cache returns error 4016 when executed

Live cache returns error – '4016 An SQL error occurred' when executed (while /SAPAPO/OM03).

It seems that live cache installation program do not create procedures in MaxDB and are not initialized properly. Is it possible to somehow initialize them manually? How do I create a clear instalation procedure?

I am currently using Platform win64, live cache version 7.4..., SCM version 4.1.

Is it easier to install & run it on win32?

✍ ANSWER

The best way to resolve this is to check initialization log and go from there. However, since you have SCM4.1 which is supported only with Live Cache 7.5, you'll have difficulty doing this even if attempted on win32. An upgrade review maybe in order to resolve the issue.

☞ Question 33

APO relevance

I am getting one warning message saying that 'work center/ resource is not APO relevant while creating integration model'. What does this mean?

✍ Answer

During the transmission of PPM, every operation of routing is checked. If a work center does not have a control key which shows that it is relevant both for capacity planning and scheduling, and both formulas are maintained in the work center to calculate capacity demand and scheduling time, the system tells you that it is not relevant for APO.

☞ QUESTION 34

Stock in transit

How to reflect the values in Intransit key figure of planning book for SNP (std). I have two location - One is shipping location A and the other one is Receiving Location.

I have created an STO IN TLB from A location and created GI. Delivery from location A STO disappeared from the location A. But I am not seeing any values in key figure in transit at location A OR B. I have an integration model for stock in transit active. How do I fix this?

✍ ANSWER

You must create an inbound delivery at the receiving location for the stock to show up being in transit. The inbound delivery is SAP's standard way of showing it in transit.

☞ Question 35

Planning book problems

I encountered two problems in my planning book design:

1) I want certain key figures to be input/output and others as output only in my data view. When I went into design view of the Planning book and right clicked on the selected key figure and made it as output, all the other key figures were also grayed out. Not trusting the design view, I checked in interactive planning and it is indeed setting all of the key figures to output only. I further checked and found there is no grouping on the key figures.

2) Typically, in interactive planning, those time buckets in the history are grayed out (output only) yet this is not occurring. I have checked my storage bucket profile and periodicities and all seem fine.

As far as I am aware this is not a GUI problem, as I am on a recent GUI patch. How do I resolve these issues?

✍ Answer

This can be fixed by going to a newer release of the GUI. Build 779065 patch 13 add on that comes with the new GUI and SCM will resolve the issues mentioned.

☞ QUESTION 36

SAP SCM Components

As far as I know SAP SCM has APO, EM and ICH as its components. However, when I checked with on-service.sap.com, it gave this list?

1. Demand and Supply Planning
2. Service Parts planning
3. Procurement
4. Manufacturing
5. Warehousing
6. Order Fulfillment
7. Transportation
8. Analytic
9. Supply Chain Event management
10. Supply Chain collaboration

I can understand that these are the processes in any supply chain. But are these all part of mySAP SCM 4.0?

✍ ANSWER

The SCM portal in SAPNet views the Supply Chain Management as the combination of the SCM components and the R3 Logistics components working together. That is the reason why when you open Procurement you get a link to Materials Management.

☞ Question 37

Extending selection conditions for prod orders in cfm1

The selection conditions for production orders do not meet the requirements of my customer when the integration model was generated. I am aware that OSS Note 507696 can be used to extend the selection criteria for MARC fields in cfm1. But information regarding this is not readily available in the production order selection. Is there a way to extend the selection criteria for production orders
(i.e. with order type AUART)? If utilizing a user exit, which one?

✍ Answer

For the first question on extending the selection criteria for production orders, I am not aware of such functions to comply with the requirement. For the second query, you can try the user exit CIFORD02 with ZXCIFU07.

☞ Question 38

✍ Answer

☞ Question 39

Periodic date Function in Macro

In my date view I got weekly buckets. I am working on a macro, wherein I need to know the week's placement in a month. The week is either the first of week of the month or the second week of the month. I saw the function which can give me the week's position in a year. However, it does not show the week's position in a month. I tried using both MONTH and WEEK function but did not yield the needed results. How can I derive the requirement of either first or second week of the month?

✍ Answer

There is no direct function to calculate this. However you can use the functions WEEK {BUCKET_BDATE (ACT_COLUMN)} for the week period requirement. Use a similar formula to place the week within the monthly period requirement. Afterwards, use EVAL to get the desired results from the above two functions.

☞ Question 40

cfm1 (integration model)

I am trying to transfer a plant from R/3 to APO but while doing so, I am getting the error:

'Error when creating address of location -- type Production plant'.

I have checked the address of the plant in R/3 but I didn't find anything wrong with it. What can be the problem and how do I resolve it?

✍ Answer

There are several ways to approach this issue. You may check any of these:

1) Have you copied the same factory calendars you are using in R/3 to APO? It is because, if they do not exist in APO it will not create the location.

2) Check the Time Zones. Ensure consistency between R/3 and APO.

3) This is a slight possibility - do you have Geo-coding set? If so, have you given the Plant the correct level to define the Geo-code in APO?

4.) Check up the region code in the location R/3. If there are special characters 'o' with a dot on top, then the plant can not be transferred to APO. There is a BW setting to permit that.

☞ Question 41

Demand Planning

We are doing implementation for Demand planning (Version 3.0A).The requirement is, they have seven (7) states for which they want to do forecasting, promotion planning, life cycle planning, etc. for each individual state based on the history data of each one. After which they want to add up the final forecast of all the states and use it for R/3. (There is no connection between R/3 and APO).

The question is, is it feasible to define seven (7) info cubes to have history data for each state and seven (7) Planning books (one for each state) to take the forecast run separately and then add up all these states' final forecast to arrive at a national level forecast? After this, the promotions will be added again at the national level to arrive for a final forecast. This will be downloaded and will be sent to R/3.

Is there a way to make it more feasible or easier to configure rather than doing the run around?

✍ Answer

To simplify things and still meet your requirements, instead of having 7 separate info cubes for each state, you can have the same results by having a single cube fed from 7 different info sources (if required). You can then have 7 planning books to control access for each state and as long as you have 'State' as a characteristic you can then forecast each state individually but still allow a higher view of the combined forecast within an overall planning book.

☞ QUESTION 42

Currency Conversion in APO DP

I want to convert the volume level data into 'Value' by converting the volume into a corresponding value. One way of doing this is by maintaining the conversion factor in the product master and setting the unit of measure in the planning book. But the problem is I want to show value in only one key figure and the rest will all be key figures that should show the volume data only. I also want to show the Key Figure in currency terms by setting the Info object Unit as currency. However, it doesn't display the same way in the planning book and shows the Planning Area UoM as the Key Figure. How can I resolve this?

A corollary question is the standard SAP demo shows value and volume information in the same planning book but I am not able to decipher how they manage to do it. How can I find a way to decipher this function?

✍ ANSWER

Try the following measures:

1) Do not define UOM for the Info object.

2) While creating the Planning area, define the UOM as currency (in the details of Key Figure, Unit of Measure column). Ideally this should allow you to use the defined Unit.

3) Ensure that you have unchecked the UOM check BOX.

4) Now write a macro to derive the value of this KF.

Reminders while doing the first four tasks:

1) When you define the KF (in which you have to put the values), define it as number and not quantity. Say this KF as KF1

2) Now while creating the Planning area, in the Key Figure TAB click details and remove UOM check Box. Next to this will be another column named "Unit of measure". Define the VALUE UOM here.

3) Save and generate the time series and the newly defined UOM will appear in planning book. However, no automatic conversion will happen here. If the conversion factors are the same, then you can write a macro to convert. Try some macros like DISPLAY_CONV_FACTOR or UNIT_CONV_FAC (I am not sure about these macros) to get the data from the product master of possible.

If the data 'quantity' is uploaded from a flat file to cube and then to PA, then you can write a small ABAP in the transfer rules to derive the value in another KF and then upload the same to PA.

☞ Question 43

Loading Purchase info into Live Cache

I have been asked to load SNP data (purchase orders) into APO 3.10 from a flat file so that the client can view it in the Planning Book [Live] SNP interactive planning/SNO plan TCODE - /SAPAPO/SDP94.

Is this possible? If so, how could is this accomplished?

✍ Answer

You can upload the information using a BAPI -BAPI_POSRVAPS_SAVEMULTI2. This can be used for the purpose but you would need the help of an ABAPer to do the task. Another option is to load them into the planning area as time series key figures and proceed from there.

☞ QUESTION 44

Changing values in a Key figure

I have a requirement from a user wherein he wants to change the values for the key figure basing on a set of drill down. The same key figure is computed by a Macro which is a default macro. Is there a way or a Macro to achieve this? If so, how is the process done?

✍ ANSWER

If you are using the standard workbook, you can make a copy of it and use that one instead. Then go to the macro workbench and change the macro so it does exactly what you want it to do.

There is a standard macro Drill down (***). Create a collective macro and put the drill down as first step. Afterwards, execute the macro. Ensure that the collective macro is the default macro.

☞ QUESTION 45

Year Dependant Fiscal Year Variant in APO DP

Our client wishes to do demand planning based on a production month calendar. The calendar is based on 12 periods per year with some periods containing 4 weeks while others contain 5 weeks. The start date and end of each period is not the same year to year. For example the "December" production month for 2005 runs from 27 Nov - 31 Dec, whereas the "December" production month for 2006 runs from 3 Dec - 30 Dec. I have created Fiscal year variants for these because the periods are not consistent year to year. I did this through the creation of a year-dependent fiscal year.

So I have managed to create the fiscal year without a problem. However, when I attempt to assign the fiscal year to the Planning Buckets profile, I get the following error:

'Input error 8 in row 1: See long text
Message no. /SAPAPO/MA 840'

Further, I managed to create the Storage buckets profile without a hitch but when I try and create time series objects for the planning area, I get this error:

'Period 2006006 is invalid for periodicity P P1
Message no. /SAPAPO/PRP104'

Diagnosis indicated that the period 2006 is not consistent with periodicity P that was entered in the storage buckets profile for the planning area. What could possibly be done to correct these errors?

✍ ANSWER

After changing the FY, make sure that you de-initialize and re-initialize your planning area. The definition of the FYV should be one year more for each in future and past period. The same applies for the initializing horizon of the planning area.

☞ Question 46

Interactive Demand Planning

Is it possible to disable the selection window in Interactive Demand Planning? I want the user to work directly with the data selection already created. Bottom line – I don't want the user to load data of his/her choice.

✍ Answer

This can be managed with authorizations. Have a look at note 400434. I think the object you are looking for is APO_SELID.

☞ Question 47

Collaborative Demand Planning

I am working on collaborative demand planning scenario in APO and need some clarification on the integration process between APO and ITS.

1. We have configured demand planning in APO and ITS has been integrated with APO system.

2. We are planning to give the access to external major customers to input and share the data.

How can this be achieved? What are the steps to be followed to achieve this?

✍ Answer

You will have to do some prior requirements:

1. First is to maintain the partner settings.

2. Second, you will have to convert your normal DP planning book into a HTML based workbook including the alerts.

3. Lastly, you should also have a collaborative planning workflow.

The second phase of the task is to do a whole of setting changes:

1. Install the Internet Transaction Server (ITS)

Before you begin with the installation, see the ITS documentation provided on the Server Components CD which is delivered together with the software.

In order to display the texts on the initial LOGON screen in the desired language, you must first set the default language in the global ITS data service using ITS parameter ~ language and the language abbreviation of the SAP system.

File Name: global.srvc

Example: ~language EN (for english text display)

Requirement: ITS version 4.6D

2. Publish the Collaborative Planning HTML templates on the ITS server.

Follow the standard procedure for publishing HTML templates together with Internet Application Components (IACs) / Easy Web Transactions (EWT). See the relevant documentation for ITS and SAP@web-studio or ABAP workbench.

The following HTML service templates are required:

CLPAMON, CLPBID, CLPGLOBAL, CLPSDP, CLPPROMCAL

The templates can be obtained in the following ways:

CAR files /File Name: 30a_apo on SAPSERV3
See OSS Note 327567 (2000)
Check out templates from APO 3.0 system using SAP@web-studio or ABAP workbench (transaction SE80).
See documentation for ITS and SAP@web-studio or ABAP workbench.

You must also install the WEBGUI and MINIALV service templates that come with the ITS installation package.

Third phase requires more setting changes:

1. General requirements for interactive Supply & Demand Planning (for ALL types of data exchange)

2. Maintain the following settings.

   2.1 Assign a planning book to the user (Demand Planning ® Environment ® Current Settings ® Assign User to Planning Book)
   See also: Planning Book Maintenance
   2.2 Assign selection profiles to the user (Demand Planning ® Environment ® Selection Organization ® Maintain Selection Assignments)
   See also: Selection Management
   2.3 Settings for drill down in the Internet planning books
   Maintain the header information of the planning view (Demand Planning ® Planning ® Interactive Demand Planning ® Settings ® Header Information).

Choose the characteristics for which you wish to enable drill down and select the Changeable indicator.

This setting must be made by the user. Otherwise the settings have no effect.

1. Display graphic in Internet planning books

2. Maintain the following data under System ® User Defaults ® Own Data on the Parameters tab page:

Parameter /sapapo/clp_webgraph, value X.

In the Internet planning book, you can then show or hide a graphical representation of your data by clicking.

If you are working with the drill down facility and wish to hide totals lines for individual key figures, click in the relevant line.

Then, use these settings for notes in Internet planning books:

→ Maintain the following data under System ® User Defaults ® Own Data on the Parameters tab page:
→ Parameter /sapapo/clp_webnote, value X

In the Internet planning book, you can then click to switch to note mode in order to enter notes on your data.

To be able to enter notes, you must use a unique selection (i.e. you must uniquely identify all characteristics).

Use these settings for the export of data:

>Maintain the following data under System ® User Defaults ® Own Data on the Parameters tab page:

Parameter /sapapo/clp_webdown, value:

XLS (if you want to process the data in Microsoft Excel)
CSV (if you want to process the data using other software)
In the Internet planning book, you can then export the data with:

Settings for sorting the data in the case of drill down
Maintain the following data under System ® User Defaults ® Own Data on the Parameters tab page:

Parameter /sapapo/clp_pivot, value X

When you have chosen drill down for a characteristic, you can then switch between the following two displays in the Internet planning book with:

Sorting of data by key figures
Sorting of data by the drill-down characteristic (e.g. product)

Settings for header lines in drill down
Maintain the following data under System ® User Defaults ® Own Data on the Parameters tab page:

Parameter /sapapo/clp_rephead, value X

The header line is then shown in the Internet planning book between the objects for which you have chosen drill down.

Choose a drill down by products and maintained the value x for the parameter /sapapo/clp_rephead. The data on the products is then separated by the header line.

Settings for header lines:

>Maintain the following data under System ® User Defaults ® Own Data on the Parameters tab page: Parameter /sapapo/clp_webbhead, value X

The header line is then repeated as a footer line in the Internet planning book.

Settings for column width:
>Maintain the following data under System ® User Defaults ® Own Data on the Parameters tab page: Parameter /sapapo/

clp_row_wi, values S, M, L, XL and ' ' (default).

This user parameter enables you to adjust the width of the fixed columns (key figure and characteristic descriptions) in the event of display problems in an Internet planning book.

Do S and M, if you want to display more columns.

This may result in the descriptions of the key figures and characteristics being incompletely displayed.

Do L and XL, if you need wider columns for more text.

Maintain APO settings for data exchange between planning books. Then, define the time series data exchange.

While APO Customizing for workflow, maintain the following Customizing settings:

→ Create users for external partners
→ Assign user names to the collaboration partners
→ Create a Collaborative Planning Workflow.
→ Supply and Demand Planning via Web access
→ Install the CLP Internet component.

If you wish to view APO alerts, see the requirements listed above.

☞ Question 48

Conversion of PP/DS PPM to SNP PPM

I am encountering complications when converting a PP/DS PPM to an SNP PPM – that is, the primary resource is not getting carried over. When I look at the SNP mode, there is duration but the Primary Resource field is blank.

The resource in question is Multimixed, and the "Not SNP Relevant" flag is not checked.

After further investigation, I called up the PP/DS PPM and did a "check plan" - which gave me several errors...namely "no bucket consumption maintained for resource"....or something to that effect.

What could be causing these errors? How can these be corrected?

✍ Answer

When the PP/DS PPM converts to a SNP PPM, it is the bucket consumption that it uses not the variable consumption that shows. You will need to add this in your PP/DS PPM.

☞ Question 49

Transferring data from R/3 to APO

I was trying to transfer data from R/3 enterprise to APO 4.0. However, even though I have inferred from help.sap.com, I still wasn't able to do this function successfully. How do I transfer data from r/3 to APO?

✍ Answer

Do the following steps:

1. Create integration models for master data and transaction data
2. Activate the integration models and select CFM1.
3. Enter the model name> select the logical system > select APO application.
   Then, select each master data and enter the relevant data for each master data.
4. After creating the model go to CFM2 to activate the model.
5. Enter the model, logical system, and the APO application.
6. Execute the transaction.

After these, you will get the model in that page. You can now select the model and activate it.

Take note that you can create location in APO or you can make one integration model for location by selecting plant in CFM1.

☞ Question 50

Changing PPMs thru BAPI_PPMSRVAPS_SAVEMULTI_30A

I want to change existing PPMs by using BAPI_PPMSRVAPS_SAVEMULTI_30A. After setting up the itabs and calling the BAPI and the necessary COMMIT WORK everything looks fine (return - table is empty). However, the values to be changed stay unmodified (checked through /SAPAPO/SCC03-transaction). With the debugger, I could find out a place in the source code where a flag is queried whether COMMIT WORK should be done inside the BAPI - after switching it on (= COMMIT WORK inside the BAPI) the new value was set and showed up in SCC03! Is there any way to turn this flag on programmatically?

If you wanted to change a field the capacity requirements structure should indicate:

*" CAPACITY_REQ STRUCTURE BAPI10003REQCAP OPTIONAL

You would also need to set an X in the corresponding entry of the additional structure (below):

*" CAPACITY_REQ_X STRUCTURE BAPI10003REQCAPX OPTIONAL

The German documentation of parameter PPM reads as if for every entry in PPM a corresponding entry in capacity_req is needed, independent of whether the capacity_req shall be changed or not. In fact, this is not true. After leaving out the capacity_req and capacity_req_x - tables, changes to the

PPMs should be accepted by the BAPI and written to the database.

✍ Answer

If you wanted to change a field the capacity requirements structure should indicate:

*" CAPACITY_REQ STRUCTURE BAPI10003REQCAP OPTIONAL

You would also need to set an X in the corresponding entry of the additional structure (below):

*" CAPACITY_REQ_X STRUCTURE BAPI10003REQCAPX OPTIONAL

The German documentation of parameter PPM reads as if for every entry in PPM a corresponding entry in capacity_req is needed, independent of whether the capacity_req shall be changed or not. In fact, this is not true. After leaving out the capacity_req and capacity_req_x - tables, changes to the PPMs should be accepted by the BAPI and written to the database.

☞ Question 51

CIF: Transferring Sales Orders from R/3 to APO

I am trying to transfer sales orders from R/3 to APO. I am able to transfer purchase orders, but not sales orders.

Once I activate the Integration Model in R/3, I am not able to see the sales order in R/3 that has to be transferred to APO.

I am looking at the right place in APO for the transferred sales orders (/SAPAPO/RRP3 - Product View). What could be the reason why sales order cannot be viewed?

✍ Answer

You need to check some items on this:

1. Check your outbound q in R/3 and inbound in APO. You will get more explanation there. May be some master data or UOM may be missing. Check the q errors first.

2. If #1 is not the problem, check whether the integration model is active and verify the inbound and out bound queues.

☞ QUESTION 52

APO Reporting

Does anyone know if there is a way to get at the APO or Live cache database via some sort of reporting tool without having to use BW?

I understand that the mySAP suite of products was designed to have all of the analytics come from BW.

✍ ANSWER

You can use Business Explorer (BeX) which loads on MS excel - needs to be setup. Or back up planning area data to a remote cube and read it using list cube.

☞ QUESTION 53

Data load into APO-DP planning book from Excel

Is it possible to load data from an Excel file into planning book in version 3.0A? I know this facility was provided in APO 4.0 onwards (readings from sap.com).

✍ ANSWER

There is an 'easy' way to do it using the normal BIW tools

1. Create a Data Target with all needed characteristics and key figures.

2. Create a Source System for a PC Flat File.

3. Create a Info source and a Info package.

Now load the Data from the CSV file into the Data Target and use transaction TSCUBE to upload the data from the Data Target into the planning area (DP).

☞ Question 54

SNP Optimizer take a lot of time running

I'm running the SNP optimizer and the solution is ok at the end, but it takes a long time in order to get the solution (around 6 hours).

We are running the optimizer for some like 4,000 SNP orders with 2 level components.

Besides to check only the required parameters in the Optimizer, what else can I do in order to shorten the planning run time?

✍ Answer

The running time depends on the optimization technique you are using. Linear is usually quicker than discretization. If you are using discretization, then the more discrete functions you use, the longer it will take. I recommend no more than 2.

☞ QUESTION 55

Saving Data in Planning Book SAP APO DP

Do you know how can I recover the Live cache data after an Initialization has been done? Is there any other option besides restoring it from the backup?

✍ ANSWER

Are you using Basis? If so, you can always rebuild it from data in your SAP APO system. It also depends on what was lost. If you lost order data (snp) and you have a connection to R3 you can rebuild almost all the results using the CIF and your R3 connected client. If it is demand planning data that is only in your dp planning area, I hope you have a back up info cube of your planning area. It is because from there, you can reload everything that was lost. If you have not yet made a back-up info cube of your planning area, then I think your best option is a system restore to a back-up.

☞ Question 56

Undoing a Live cache Initialization

Why is the data not saved in the key figure when the dis-aggregation type is set to "N" (No dis-aggregation) in the planning area? Each time the 'save' button is clicked in the planning book, the data is lost.

✍ Answer

If you have dis-aggregation turned off, the only place you can save data would be at the lowest level. Figure out where your lowest level is and you're your data there.

Or you could also try to save data at the level that you had an aggregate function.

☞ Question 57

Product Planning Table set up

I'm working with APO 3.0. Using transaction /SAPAPO/PPT1 (Product planning table) on screen "Product view: periodic" some PlOrd rows are modifiable (input/output) while some are not (output only). The PPMs are different. PlOrd-s with input possibility connects to different resources than others. I want to modify all PlOrd quantity. What is missing here?

✍ Answer

Check the resource operating time assigned to resource. The planed orders connecting to resource are used as output only in the planning table if no time is assigned.

☞ Question 58

One or more planning areas/book in DP

I have 10 different countries set up in my system. Each of them has their own demand planners. I have set up a planning area and a planning book for one of them and my idea is to set up identical planning books and areas for the rest. The result will then to produce 10 different planning areas with the same exact structure.

I want to know if that is the best practice (or option), or shall I try to set up just one planning area for all of them? If so, are the users going to be blocked when they start working?

✍ Answer

I would recommend one planning area/book. You can control who accesses data via the selection profiles. As long as the selection profiles don't overlap, the users will not be able to lock each other out.

There are some things that you have to look out for though:

1) If there is any change in process requested by a single country it would become difficult to manage considering the fact that all other countries also share the same configuration.

2) Using a single planning area and POS will also increase the CVCs handled and can cause a lag in performance.

3) The data management will be a bit tricky and functions like realignment (if required) should be handled carefully.

4) Impact of mismanagement (scheduling a wrong background job for instance) would me on higher side with such set of configuration.

Given the above, you can evaluate the pros and cons of both approaches and go from there.

☞ QUESTION 59

Assigning characteristic value for PPMs via CIF

I'm trying to find a way to automatically assign characteristics to the PPMs when CIF occurs. How can this be done?

✍ ANSWER

Try developing a user exit for the note 495825.

☞ Question 60

SNP standard planning areas- issues

I encountered some issues while doing SNP standard planning areas:

1) The default UOM assigned to 9aSNP02 is PC, we don't use that unit of measure. What is the best option to go about it? I need to create a new planning area of 9aSNP02.

2) When we initialize 9asnp02 it doesn't ask for a date from and to, like it does for 9aSNP01. Is this normal?

3) Initialization of 9asnp01 takes a long time while 9asnp02 is done in a few minutes. Why so?

✍ Answer

The responses are numbered accordingly:

1.) Yes. Create a copy of the 9ASNP02 planning area and change the default UoM.

2.) The planning area 9ASNP02 is an order based planning area and therefore doesn't require a time series like 9ASNP01.

3.) This is related to the generation of time series (see response to number 2).

☞ Question 61

APO -DP Inability to track quantity changes in forecasts

APO - Demand Planning

Does anyone know if there is a method to track quantity changes in forecasts? When a person changes an entry in a planning book, the system does not automatically create a historical record of the change. Does anyone know if there is a way to handle the changes?

✍ Answer

There can be two (or more) solutions, depending on your exact requirement.

If you need to capture the how, what, and when of a forecast change, you'll need audit trail functionality. Although no such functionality exists out of the box, it can be developed using macros. You can create a default macro that validates whether a key figure value has changed. If it does change, you can create an entry in a z-table that records the original value, the new value, the user, and the date (or any other data you might need). Then create a BW report that reports this data.

If you just need to capture the values of all key figures at a periodic interval, extract the planning area contents to an Info Cube. By using a timestamp for the extraction period, you can run reports that compare the values of key figures during points in time. This is normally called a waterfall report.

☞ Question 62

Key figures in Planning book

I have created a Planning book with all custom key figures.

I want certain key figures to be input/output and others as output only (so that they are grayed out in the book). When I went into design view of the Planning book (from the planning book) and right clicked on the selected key figure and made it as output only I was surprised to see that all the other key figures also were grayed out (in the sense, the input output key figures that really needs to be made as input key figure was also grayed out). I checked and there is no grouping. Is there any grouping at Planning book level for key figures?

✍ Answer

You should have the latest SAPGUI patches and SCM Add-in patches. This will solve the problem.

☞ Question 63

ATP Horizon

Any idea where we can define the ATP horizon? For example, the period for which ATP check would be carried out. I believe it must be somewhere while initializing the ATP time series. Where can I find this function and how should we go about it?

✍ Answer

The ATP Checking Horizon is defined per product/location combination in the Checking Horizon Field on the product master. Remember to use an ATP Group that takes the horizon into account

☞ Question 64

Dynamic pegging

How do we change the dynamic pegging relationship interactively?

My problem is I have stocks dynamically pegged to say sales order no 1.

Later on I have a sales order no. 2 which is to be confirmed and delivered before sales order no 1. The system doesn't confirm any quantities due to the fact that the quantities are dynamically pegged to sales order no1.

How can I change the dynamic pegging relation?

✍ Answer

You can do it from product view. Double click on element to go to details. Over there you can see the details of pegging relationship, and you can also see alternatives for pegging, which you can fix.

From your description though, it seems this is not a pegging issue, but an ATP issue. If the above does not work for you, try using Tcode /SAPAPO/BOPI to switch confirmation from one order to another (If you are using Global-ATP, otherwise you should use CO06 in R/3).

☞ QUESTION 65

LOADING TEXT AND MASTER DATA

I have encountered some difficulties regarding uploading text and master data in BW Info Object. My client wants to create his own report on the BW embedded on APO (3.0).

For example, 9ALOCNO has the code but contains no description nor attributes. What kind of activity is necessary for it to work in APO? Do I have to create a custom data source reading /SAPAPO/* tables?

✍ ANSWER

You can load text since 9ALOCNO has a text table. But you can't load any attributes. It is because 9ALOCNO does not have any attributes in its definition.

☞ Question 66

/SAPAPO/TSM 219: Invalid Data Status

When I try to load a particular product group in the planning book, I am getting the following Error Message. This happens only for 3 product groups but it works fine for the rest of the other product groups:

'/SAPAPO/TSM 219: Invalid Data Status.'

This Error should not occur during normal processing. If it does occur, contact the System Administration or call the SAP Hotline Number.

Application Area: /SAPAPO/TSM
Message No: 219

Is this a functional/configuration/master data problem or does it have something to do with System Administration or support packs?

✍ Answer

There are numerous reasons why this can occur. Data inconsistencies in the system are usually the main culprit. The solution will depend on the exact functionality that is causing the message and also your APO release/service pack.

The best bet for you is to go onto SAP service place and do a notes search on that error message number and then apply the notes that are relevant for your release/patch level.

Usually the construction check program repairs the LC errors with invalid data status. Run the program /SAPAPO/TS_LCM_CONS_CHECK with the 'Repair' option.

☞ Question 67

User Exit for /SAPAPO/TS_PLOBS_ GENERATE

In order to create Character Combinations (CC) in the background, it is possible to use the standard report "/ SAPAPO/TS_PLOBS_GENERATE" on the basis of an info cube.

The report also offers obviously the possibility to use a user exit. However, I can't find the right user-exit. Where can I find the right user exit?

✍ Answer

Use the BADI: /SAPAPO/SDP_MASTER exit for your purpose.

☞ QUESTION 68

Forecast in weeks and months

My time bucket profile is 12 months of which the first three months are in weeks and the rest are indicated in months. The last week of the current month is common between current month and next month.

For example:

Technically the last day of week 4 of August 2005 is September 2005. How can we make the system consider Aug 31st as the last day of week 4 and Sept 1st as the beginning of the new week?

✍ ANSWER

You can use the fiscal year variants and associate them with your storage bucket profile. This will produce the results you are looking for.

☞ QUESTION 69

Blocked stock in APO

We are implementing APO 3.1 with SAP R/3 4.7. Blocked stock is not recognized in APO 3.1 as available stock. I know that it is recognized in 4.x but we can't upgrade to 4.x at present. So, I am looking for some help. How do I resolve the blocked stock in 3.1?

✍ ANSWER

You can use the exit described in note 487166 for enhancement of APOCF011.

☞ QUESTION 70

Classification view of Product master in APO

We would like to use the Characteristics in the Classification view of the product master in APO. Normally, when I create a characteristic in R/3 and attach it to a class within the classification view of the Material master, the relevant characteristic will be displayed out - of which I can select a value.

For example:

If my Characteristic is color that I have attached to a class, when this class is called in the Classification view of the Material master, the Characteristic is called in which I can either select RED or YELLOW etc. But in APO, I have done the same thing by creating a Characteristic, attaching it to a Class. However, when I called the Class in Classification view of the product master and clicked the details icon, I see only the Characteristic Name (but not the values) which means that I cannot assign a value to that particular part number (product) in APO.

I am not sure where I went wrong in any step. How do I determine where I went wrong and how can I fix this?

Note that I have tried transferring the Class & Characteristics using CIF - that too didn't work. We are in APO3.1.

✍ ANSWER

You need to maintain the Customizing in R/3 and the same in APO as the Customizing are not CIFed throughout the Integration models.

Please enter the organizational area at the level of the Class and at the level of individual characteristic identifying it as those that are supposed to go to APO.

In APO, select the table /SAPAPO/MATKEY and choose Organizational Areas.

Choose 'new Entries' to create organizational areas. If you have not maintained the system, it will still transfer but you may not be able to display the input.

These things are primarily done since these customizing are not transferred through CIF.

☞ Question 71

Stop live cache versus stopSAP

My question is regarding the activation of a parameter change in Live cache.

Will stopping (stopSAP ALL) SAP have the same effect as stopping Live cache to activate the parameter change? Or is it entirely different?

Do changes to Live cache parameter require stop&start Live cache only? Can it possibly be activated even after a stopSAP?

✍ Answer

If you restart just the lc, then that is all you do - restart the Live cache.

If you do a 'stopSAP ALL' then it depends:

As of SCM 40, then everything is stopped, including lc. However, be careful with earlier SCM/APO versions - only the app server and underlying database (i.e. oracle) is actually stopped - the Live cache is still there.

You should have no reason to restart the whole system just to activate some lc parameter changes. Simply use the functionality in LC10. It is also safer than using the DBMGUI (especially with older lc / APO versions).

☞ QUESTION 72

Live Cache to APO tables

I need to know if there is a function modules/BADI that reads the data from Live cache to APO tables.

For Example:

How does the SA line derive from the Live cache and stored in transparent table?

✍ ANSWER

COM routines are called from the ABAP function modules to perform actions on any lc data which is stored in the object oriented data areas. For all other (relational) data you can use native SQL calls.

If you want to view the lc data you can use /SAPAPO/OM16.

☞ QUESTION 73

Connection between Live cache & BW

We have separate Live cache server, APO server and BW server. The process we follow now is that after running different programs in Live cache for demand planning, we load the data to a cube (say cube xyz) in the APO server for back up of the Live cache data. We then load the data from cube xyz from the APO server to a cube in BW server for reporting.

Is there a way to load data directly from the Live cache to BW, without loading the APO server? If yes, what do I need to do in Live cache to set up the connection to BW?

✍ ANSWER

You need to define your planning area in APO as a data source for BW. IN APO, run transaction /SAPAPO/MSDP_ADMIN and right click on your planning area. Use option 'generate data source'. In BW, in transaction RSA1, select APO as your source system, replicate to see the data source you have just created and build your system from there on.

However, if you mean connecting the Live cache directly to the BW system, instead of saving the planning results into the local APO system then copying them across to the remote cube, then No, you definitely can't!!!

☞ Question 74

Stock in transit Upload

Can anyone tell me what BAPI or RFC can be used to upload Stock in transit data from the External source?

✍ Answer

Take BAPI_GOODSMVT_CREATE plus an integration model.

Stock would be entered into the R/3 system via a goods movement created by the above BAPI and an integration model would transfer the stock information to APO.

☞ Question 75

Changing a resource in a Heuristic

I am using a Customer Heuristics in which I change the resource for a specific order operation before the Function "/SAPAPO/EFPL_ONLINE_SCHEDULER" is called.

When I debug the Function I noticed it calls another Function "/SAPAPO/OM_ACT_SCHEDULE". This function in turn connects to Live Cache & calls the stored procedure "SAPAPO_PT_ACT_SCHEDULE2" with the changed resource data. However, it schedules the order operation with the wrong resource.

I assume that the stored procedure uses the resource data found in Live Cache and not the data passed to it by the last Function.

How do I solve this problem?

My first guess is to change the order prior to calling the "/SAPAPO/EFPL_ONLINE_SCHEDULER" Function.

What function do I use (if at all) to change the order?

✍ Answer

In the Internal Table containing the Capacity Requirements, you should also change the MODE_NO to -1 prior to calling the online schedular (/SAPAPO/EFPL_ONLINE_SCHEDULAR).

INDEX

Attention SAP Experts

50% Off your next SAPCOOKBOOK order

Interview books are great for cross-training

In the new global economy, the more you know the better. The sharpest consultants are doing everything they can to pick up more than one functional area of SAP. Each of the following Certification Review / Interview Question books provides an excellent starting point for your module learning and investigation. These books get you started like no other book can – by providing you the information that you really need to know, and fast.

SAPCOOKBOOK Interview Questions, Answers, and Explanations

ABAP -	SAP ABAP Certification Review: SAP ABAP Interview Questions, Answers, and Explanations
SD -	SAP SD Interview Questions, Answers, and Explanations
Security -	SAP Security: SAP Security Essentials
HR -	mySAP HR Interview Questions, Answers, and Explanations: SAP HR Certification Review
BW -	SAP BW Ultimate Interview Questions, Answers, and Explanations: SAW BW Certification Review
-	SAP SRM Interview Questions Answers and Explanations
Basis -	SAPBasisCertificationQuestions:BasisInterview Questions, Answers, and Explanations
MM -	SAP MM Certification and Interview Questions: SAP MM Interview Questions, Answers, and Explanations

SAP BW Ultimate Interview Questions, Answers, and Explanations

Key Topics Include:

- The most important BW settings to know
- BW tables and transaction code quick references
- Certification Examination Questions
- Extraction, Modeling and Configuration
- Transformations and Administration
- Performance Tuning, Tips & Tricks, and FAQ
- Everything a BW resource needs to know before an interview

mySAP HR Interview Questions, Answers, and Explanations

Key topics include:

- The most important HR settings to know
- mySAP HR Administration tables and transaction code quick references
- SAP HR Certification Examination Questions
- Org plan, Compensation, Year End, Wages, and Taxes
- User Management, Transport System, Patches, and Upgrades
- Benefits, Holidays, Payroll, and Infotypes
- Everything an HR resource needs to know before an interview

SAP SRM Interview Questions, Answers, and Explanations

Key Topics Include:

- The most important SRM Configuration to know
- Common EBP Implementation Scenarios
- Purchasing Document Approval Processes
- Supplier Self Registration and Self Service (SUS)
- Live Auctions and Bidding Engine, RFX Processes (LAC)
- Details for Business Intelligence and Spend Analysis
- EBP Technical and Troubleshooting Information

SAP MM Interview Questions, Answers, and Explanations

- The most important MM Configuration to know
- Common MM Implementation Scenarios
- MM Certification Exam Questions
- Consumption Based Planning
- Warehouse Management
- Material Master Creation and Planning
- Purchasing Document Inforecords

SAP SD Interview Questions, Answers, and Explanations

- The most important SD settings to know
- SAP SD administration tables and transaction code quick references
- SAP SD Certification Examination Questions
- Sales Organization and Document Flow Introduction
- Partner Procedures, Backorder Processing, Sales BOM
- Backorder Processing, Third Party Ordering, Rebates and Refunds
- Everything an SD resource needs to know before an interview

SAP Basis Interview Questions, Answers, and Explanations

- The most important Basis settings to know
- Basis Administration tables and transaction code quick references
- Certification Examination Questions
- Oracle database, UNIX, and MS Windows Technical Information
- User Management, Transport System, Patches, and Upgrades
- Backup and Restore, Archiving, Disaster Recover, and Security
- Everything a Basis resource needs to know before an interview

SAP Security Essentials

- Finding Audit Critical Combinations
- Authentication, Transaction Logging, and Passwords
- Roles, Profiles, and User Management
- ITAR, DCAA, DCMA, and Audit Requirements
- The most important security settings to know
- Security Tuning, Tips & Tricks, and FAQ
- Transaction code list and table name references

SAP Workflow Interview Questions, Answers, and Explanations

- Database Updates and Changing the Standard
- List Processing, Internal Tables, and ALV Grid Control
- Dialog Programming, ABAP Objects
- Data Transfer, Basis Administration
- ABAP Development reference updated for 2006!
- Everything an ABAP resource needs to know before an interview

www.ingramcontent.com/pod-product-compliance
Ingram Content Group UK Ltd.
Pitfield, Milton Keynes, MK11 3LW, UK
UKHW040227290926
15471UKWH00001B/34

9 781933 804088